CONTROLS
AND IMPEDIMENTS AFFECTING
INWARD DIRECT INVESTMENT

IN OECD MEMBER COUNTRIES

ORGANISATION FOR ECONOMIC CO-OPERATION AND DEVELOPMENT

The Organisation for Economic Co-operation and Development (OECD) was set up under a Convention signed in Paris on 14th December 1960, which provides that the OECD shall promote policies designed:

- to achieve the highest sustainable economic growth and employment and a rising standard of living in Member countries, while maintaining financial stability, and thus to contribute to the development of the world economy;
- to contribute to sound economic expansion in Member as well as non-member countries in the process of economic development;
- to contribute to the expansion of world trade on a multilateral, non-discriminatory basis in accordance with international obligations.

The Members of OECD are Australia, Austria, Belgium, Canada, Denmark, Finland, France, the Federal Republic of Germany, Greece, Iceland, Ireland, Italy, Japan, Luxembourg, the Netherlands, New Zealand, Norway, Portugal, Spain, Sweden, Switzerland, Turkey, the United Kingdom and the United States.

Publié en français sous le titre

CONTROLES ET OBSTACLES AUX INVESTISSEMENTS DIRECTS DE L'ÉTRANGER
DANS LES PAYS MEMBRES DE L'OCDE

.˙.

A significant proportion of the work of OECD's Committee on Capital Movements and Invisible Transactions has focused on the application of the Code of Liberalisation of Capital Movements to direct investment, in particular inward direct investment. One reason for this is the significant role played by international direct investment in furthering the growth and interdependence of the OECD economies.

The Committee's work shows the complexity of issues relating to Member country policies, laws, regulations and administrative practices relating to inward direct investment operations.

This is why the Committee collects information regularly from Member countries in order to achieve greater transparency and closer international co-operation in this field.

The present study presents the results of the latest survey carried out by the Committee and gives a picture of the laws, regulations and administrative practices with regard to inward direct investment in Member countries at end-June, 1981. The study is not limited to restrictions in the sense of the Code of Liberalisation but also deals with other categories of obstacles; it covers restrictions, controls and other general impediments, sectoral controls and obstacles, and gives information on monopolies and the sectors where they apply as well as on the regulations on access to the domestic capital market by non-resident investors.

Also available

INTERNATIONAL INVESTMENT AND MULTINATIONAL ENTERPRISES.
Revised edition 1979 (January 1980)
(21 80 01 1) ISBN 92-64-12023-8   32 pages   £1.30   US$3.00   F12.00

CONTROLS ON INTERNATIONAL CAPITAL MOVEMENTS: Experience with
controls on international portfolio operations in shares and bonds (January 1981)
(21 80 07 1) ISBN 92-64-12138-2   64 pages   £2.80   US$7.00   F28.00

INTERNATIONAL INVESTMENT AND MULTINATIONAL ENTERPRISES:
Recent International Investment Trends (October 1981)
(21 81 03 1) ISBN 92-64-12250-8   108 pages   £4.60   US$10.00   F46.00

FOREIGN INVESTMENT IN YUGOSLAVIA (February 1982)
(21 82 01 1) ISBN 92-64-12273-7   72 pages   £2.70   US$6.00   F27.00

CODE OF LIBERALISATION OF CAPITAL MOVEMENTS – March 1982
Edition (April 1982)
(21 82 04 1) ISBN 92-64-12070-X   106 pages   £4.90   US$11.00   F49.00

Prices charged at the OECD Publications Office.

*THE OECD CATALOGUE OF PUBLICATIONS and supplements will be sent free of charge
on request addressed either to OECD Publications Office,
2, rue André-Pascal, 75775 PARIS CEDEX 16, or to the OECD Sales Agent in your country.*

TABLE OF CONTENTS

I. INTRODUCTION

A. BACKGROUND

1.   The OECD countries agreed when the Organisation was established in 1960 that the free international movement of private capital flows is generally a desirable objective in that such capital movements promote a more efficient utilisation of available economic resources. The OECD's Convention thus states that Members will "pursue their efforts to extend the liberalisation of capital movements", and this principle was embodied in 1961 in a legal instrument, the Code of Liberalisation of Capital Movements (hereafter called "the Code") to which all Member countries except Canada adhere. One of the most important capital movements covered by the Code is Direct Investment, which is defined as "investment for the purpose of establishing lasting economic relations with an undertaking such as, in particular, investments which give the possibility of exercising an effective influence on the management thereof". The liberalisation obligations of the Code require the authorities concerned to authorise automatically transactions and transfers involving international direct investment to or from other OECD countries and to allow the proceeds of its liquidation to be re-transferred. Subject to certain limited provisos in the Articles of the Code, this obligation is reduced only to the extent that some Member countries have a dispensation (reservation or derogation) with respect to some or all of these items.

2.   OECD's Committee on Capital Movements and Invisible Transactions (hereafter called "the Committee"), composed of independent experts nominated by Member countries, has been entrusted with surveillance of the application of the Code. This task includes, in particular, undertaking periodic reviews of the reservations or derogations Member countries maintain with respect to their liberalisation obligations, examining the justifications of the restrictive measures in question in light of changing circumstances (e.g. the economic and financial positions of the countries) and, where appropriate, recommending that certain measures be relaxed or dropped.

3.   A significant proportion of the Committee's work during the past two decades has focused on the application of the Code to direct investment, in particular, inward direct investment. One reason for this is the significant role played by international direct investment in furthering the growth and interdependence of the OECD economies. This was underlined at the 1976 Meeting of the OECD Council at Ministerial level when the Member governments stated in their Declaration on International Investment and Multinational Enterprises that "international investment has assumed increased importance in the world economy and has considerably contributed to the development of their countries", which was reaffirmed in the 1979

Ministerial Meeting(1). The Committee's extensive work on applying the Code to inward direct investment also reflects the complexity and in some cases the difficulty of issues relating to Member country policies, laws, regulations and administrative practices relating to inward direct investment operations. It is an area where a high degree of liberalisation has been achieved in Member countries under the Code with respect to the treatment of direct investment capital transactions and transfers and yet where a number of restrictions remain. Moreover, there are a considerable number of other measures which, while not falling under the liberalisation obligations of the Code, do represent obstacles or limitations on the ability of foreign investors to undertake certain investments and carry out business activities.

4.   While information on most of these measures is in the public domain, it is scattered in many places due to the diversity of government agencies involved in most cases; therefore the Committee determined that, in the interests of increased transparency and international co-operation, it would be highly desirable to develop systematically a comprehensive and accurate picture of the various laws, regulations and administrative practices which affect the ability of non-residents to undertake direct investments in Member countries. This picture was prepared through a survey prepared by the Member governments. This report presents the results of that survey and gives a picture of the situation which existed at end-June 1981. It thus represents an updating and supplement to the information on inward investment measures in the Committee's previous study on direct investment policies, procedures and practices(2). It should be noted that this report, as the previous study, does not contain any information on Iceland and Turkey and that the information concerning Canada and Greece, and relating in particular to concessions, licence requirements, and public, private, or mixed monopolies, is not complete.

B. SCOPE OF THE SURVEY

5.   The detailed information provided by the survey is presented on a country-by-country basis in the three tables annexed to this report. Table I gives lists of controls and impediments of a general nature, that is, measures that do not refer to specific sectors. These include restrictions of a general nature which are covered by Member country reservations or derogations to the Code, as well as other general measures which may constitute impediments to inward direct investment. Where applicable, brief descriptions of existing authorisation procedures for inward direct investment are given. Table II lists restrictions on local financing of inward direct investment and thus concerns conditions relating to the access of non-resident investors to domestic capital markets. These measures also are of a general nature but are drawn together here for separate analysis. Finally, Table III lists controls and impediments to inward direct investment which apply to specific sectors. As in Table I, this table includes both restrictions covered by Member country reservations or derogations to the Code and other sector-specific measures which may constitute impediments to direct investment in those sectors. Table III therefore includes the numerous impediments non-residents may

---

1. International Investment and Multinational Enterprises, Revised Edition, 1979, OECD, and also International Investment and Multinational Enterprises: Review of the 1976 Declaration and Decisions, 1979, OECD.
    2. International Direct Investment: Policies, Procedures and Practices in OECD Member Countries, 1979, OECD.

encounter in seeking to invest and carry out business activities in industries subject to a high degree of regulation in Member countries, most of
which are found in the service sector. To provide a complete picture, the
table includes the obstacles presented by the existence of public, private
or mixed monopolies in certain sectors.

6. In order to understand better the classification of information within the three tables, several comments on the scope of the Code's liberalisation obligations with respect to direct investment should be made. Certain limitations on the coverage of the survey should also be noted.
First, with respect to those measures which relate to the legal establishment of an enterprise in a sector, the Code does not confer the "right of
establishment" except where there are certain elements of this right
expressly provided for in the Code. In addition to the rights noted
earlier to carry out capital transactions and transfers related to inward
direct investment and subsequently liquidate the resulting investment, the
Code also provides for the right of a non-resident parent, after establishing a subsidiary or branch, to extend these enterprises and to have
its securities admitted to the capital markets of the country of investment. The parent and its subsidiary or branch are also to enjoy the
liberalisation of such additional operations as credits directly linked
with international commercial transactions or with the rendering of international services, financial credits and loans, sureties and guarantees,
and physical movements of capital assets. But the "right of establishment" is generally understood to include numerous further rights relating
to the right to set up and manage undertakings under the conditions laid
down for its own nationals by the law of the country where such establishment is effected. As can be seen from the measures listed in the second
column of Table I, those in Table II and, most importantly, those in the
second and third columns of Table III, there are a number of measures not
covered by reservations or derogations to the Code which can present obstacles to foreign investors, particularly within certain industries in
the service sectors of Member country economies(3).

7. The Code, of course, does not entitle a non-resident to engage in an
economic activity without compliance with the general regulations of the
governments concerned; it does not confer on non-residents a claim to pre-
ferential treatment over residents. For similar reasons, this survey ex-
cludes concession or licence requirements and regulations applying to the
modality of operations which use the same standards for or apply equally
to resident and non-resident investors. Rather, the survey examines those
concession or licensing requirements or regulations applying to the
modalities of operations which specifically raise special barriers or
limitations to the access of non-resident investors (as compared with
resident investors) to the establishment and operation of business enterprises in specific sectors.

8. The liberalisation obligations of the Code do not encompass measures
taken for the protection of public order or essential security

---

3. Obstacles, controls and other impediments affecting investment by
foreign controlled enterprises established in the country concerned are
not covered here, as they relate to the chapter on National Treatment of
the 1976 Declaration and Decisions on International Investment and Multinational Enterprises, op. cit. This chapter also includes other aspects
of treatment of foreign controlled companies established in the country
concerned. The latest available survey in this area is the OECD publication "National treatment of foreign controlled enterprises established in
OECD Member countries" 1978.

interests(4). The liberalisation obligations of the Code similarly are not breached by measures preventing an investment when, in the view of the Member government concerned, that investment would have an exceptionally detrimental effect on the interests of the Member country concerned(5). In both cases the interpretation of the applicability of relevant exceptions in the Code are left to the judgment of the Member country concerned, but in the case of the latter exception, the Organisation is to be notified of each instance where an envisaged investment is refused on this basis. The survey does not specifically identify measures taken under those two qualifications to the Code's liberalisation obligations.

---

4. See the OECD Code of Liberalisation of Capital Movements, Article 3.
5. See the OECD Code of Liberalisation of Capital Movements; Remark (ii) to Item I, List A, Annex A.

II. OVERVIEW OF SURVEY RESULTS

A. RESTRICTIONS, CONTROLS AND OTHER GENERAL IMPEDIMENTS

9.   Of the 11 Member countries which currently maintain under the Code full or limited reservations on the inward direct investment item, the underlying measures in six of these countries (Australia, Austria, Finland, New Zealand, Portugal, Spain) are, at least in part, of a general nature. Most of these measures involve authorisation requirements which are not specific to certain sectors, although they are frequently limited in other ways. As these procedures are detailed in the Committee's report "International Direct Investment Policies, Procedures and Practices in OECD Member Countries", they are described in only very summary form here, except in two cases where there have been recent changes in these procedures.

10.   Formal authorisation procedures exist in all but six Member countries (Germany, Italy, Netherlands, Switzerland, United Kingdom, and the United States), but the scope of application and the restrictiveness of these procedures varies considerably from country to country. Prior authorisation for all inward direct investments by non-residents is required in Austria, Finland, Greece, Ireland, New Zealand, Norway, Portugal and Sweden. In addition, all direct investments by foreign-controlled resident enterprises also require authorisation in Finland, New Zealand, Norway and Portugal.

11.   In Australia, prior authorisation is required for certain investments, by foreign interests irrespective of whether a capital inflow would be involved(6). In Canada, authorisation under the Foreign Investment Review Act is required when the investment applies to the acquisition of control of an existing Canadian business enterprise in Canada, either by foreign persons who do not already have an existing business in Canada or by foreign persons in Canada, if the new business is unrelated to the existing business. In Denmark, authorisation is required only when the total foreign investment in the enterprises exceeds Kroner 1 million per calendar year or the investment is made in an enterprise the object of which exclusively or to any considerable extent is to carry on capital investments abroad or the financing of non-residents, or the investment is made by a foreign enterprise in which a resident directly or indirectly possesses assets representing a direct investment. In Spain, authorisation is required as a general rule for foreign investments in Spanish firms in excess of 50 per cent of the capital of those firms.

----

6. A full description of Australia's foreign investment policy is given in Your Investment in Australia: A Guide for Investors, 1981, pages 7-15, 28-41.

12. In two countries, recent changes in authorisation procedures should be noted. In Japan, under the 1980 amendment to the Foreign Exchange and Foreign Trade Control Law the former authorisation system has been transformed into a prior notification system for inward direct investment. A foreign investor is obliged to give prior notice to the Minister of Finance and the Minister(s) in charge of the industry concerned. He is free to invest after two weeks, in principle. However, in some exceptional cases, the Minister of Finance and Minister(s) concerned may recommend or order an amendment of the contents of the transaction or its suspension. In particular, there would be cases where such an investment might generate the following results:

a) it might imperil national security, disturb order or the safety of the general public; or
b) it might adversely and seriously affect the activity of the industry engaging in business similar to the one in which the direct investment is to be made, or it might imperil the smooth functioning of the national economy.

In practice, criterion (b) would be applied to the four specific industries on which Japan has a reservation in the Code (agriculture, forestries and fisheries; mining; oil; and leather and leather products manufacturing) and to cases corresponding to the exception cited in Remark (ii) to Item 1, List A, Annex A, of the Code, noted in paragraph 8 above.

13. In France, authorisation procedures also were modified in 1980 and now incorporate the following distinctions:

a) For inward direct investments from non-EEC countries, prior authorisation of the Ministry of Economics is normally required, whether the investment is made by non-residents or by French companies under foreign control. The following operations, however, do not require prior authorisation provided they are financed by means of foreign currency:

  - up to Frs.5 million per calendar year: new investment in French enterprises by non-residents who have already been authorised to participate in them provided that the new operation does not increase the percentage of their participation;
  - up to Frs.5 million per calendar year: purchasing or setting up handicraft or retail trade enterprises to be operated by the non-resident investor himself;
  - without limitation: setting-up of real estate enterprises.

b) For inward direct investment from EEC member countries, only prior notification is required, except in the following cases (which do require authorisation):

  - investment by enterprises controlled by residents of non-EEC member countries;
  - investment in sectors of activity which participate in France, even only occasionally, in the administration of public authority;
  - investment affecting public order, health, or security as well as investment in activities related to the production of or trading in weapons, ammunition and war material;
  - operations the effect of which would be to obstruct the application of French laws and regulations.

The French authorities have indicated that in some exceptional cases of investment from non-EEC member countries, they use their powers to restrict

restrict investments where in view of the amount involved or of other factors a specific transaction or transfer would have an exceptionally detrimental effect on the interests of France, which is the exception provided by Remark (ii) to Item I, List A, Annex A, of the Code.

14.   The remaining general impediments to inward direct investment, listed in the third column of Table I, are relatively few in number.   In Norway, foreigners and foreign-controlled companies (defined as companies where more than 20 per cent of the voting rights or the share of capital is owned by foreigners or foreign-controlled companies, or where at least one member of the Board is an alien) must have a concession for purchases of real property.   Furthermore, foreigners and foreign-controlled companies must have a concession to acquire more than 10 per cent of the share capital of a company owning or leasing real property.   To obtain this concession, it is usually required that the Chairman and the majority of the Board of Directors be Norwegian citizens, and that the transactions between the Norwegian subsidiary and its foreign parent are based upon realistic pricing and optimum conditions for the Norwegian company.   The conditions may also regulate the type of production, financing terms and other circumstances varying from company to company.   Also, a concession is necessary to purchase electric power in larger quantities than 1000 k.w.   If the concessionaire is a company with an Executive Board which is not entirely Norwegian-held, the State may in the concession terms reserve a right to purchase, not later than 40 years from the concession date, the factory plants established for the purpose of utilising the power, together with land, buildings, machinery, facilities, etc. Finally, the Joint Stock Companies Act of 4th June, 1976 requires that the manager in a joint stock company, at least half the members of the Board of Directors, the corporate assembly and the Committee of Representatives be permanently resident in Norway.   In Sweden, aliens and foreign corporations must also have a special permit to acquire real property.   In order to prevent an alien or a foreign corporation from acquiring real property through the acquisition of shares of a Swedish company which owns real property, aliens and foreign corporations, as well as Swedish corporations without a foreigners' clause in their Articles of Association, may not acquire non-free shares, i.e. those tied to Swedish nationals by virtue of a restricting clause.   This means that at most 20 per cent of voting rights and 40 per cent of the share capital can be acquired in the absence of such a clause.   The removal of such clauses is subject to authorisation.   Furthermore, aliens, foreign corporations and Swedish limited companies with the status of foreign corporations may not without a special permit take part in trading partnerships.   In Switzerland, the Board of Joint Stock Companies, with the exception of holding companies, must include a majority of persons residing in Switzerland and of Swiss nationality.

15.   Switzerland also has restrictions concerning foreign ownership of buildings, and Australia, Finland and New Zealand also are listed as having restrictions concerning foreign ownership of buildings.   In addition to these countries, seven additional Member countries, Austria, Denmark, Japan, Norway, Portugal, Spain and Sweden, have restrictions on the building or purchase of real estate by non-residents, which are covered by reservations on this item in the Code.   Also, in the United States there are legislations restricting at the State level the acquisition of land by non-resident foreigners or foreign corporations in some States.

16.   Restrictions on local financing of inward direct investment, while also of a general nature, have been drawn together and listed in Table II, giving restrictions on the local financing of a new foreign-controlled enterprise.   The following general observations might be made on this table:

i) there is a sizeable group of Member countries, among them some of the largest recipients (as well as originators) of international direct investment, which do not distinguish between resident and non-resident investors when it comes to raising funds in the domestic capital markets (for instance, Canada, Germany, Japan, Luxembourg, the Netherlands, Switzerland, the United Kingdom and the United States);

ii) however, a large number of Member countries restrict the access to the local capital market of non-residents for the purpose of direct investment in their territories or in a way that may affect the financing of direct investment in their territories (for instance, Australia, Austria, Belgium, Denmark, Finland, France, Italy, New Zealand, Norway, Portugal, Spain and Sweden). The degree of restrictive effect varies substantially between these countries.

B. SECTORAL CONTROLS AND OBSTACLES

17. Sectoral controls and/or obstacles to inward foreign investment including those relating to reservations in Annex B to the Code of Liberalisation of Capital Movements involve a wide variety of industries. A number of countries refer specifically, in their reservations, to the sectors or industries where restrictions to liberalisation obligations of the Code are applied (Ireland: flour milling; Japan: primary industries related to agriculture, forestry and fisheries; mining, oil, leather and leather products manufacturing; Spain: film and information; United States: specified limitations to investment by aliens in enterprises engaged in fresh water shipping, domestic radio, communications, domestic air transport etc.). Other countries (Finland, Norway, Sweden) do not refer to specific sectors but indicate that their reservations apply to the extent that there are limitations on the right of foreigners to engage in certain activities or to acquire, own or lease certain types of property.

18. As is shown in Table III, other controls and impediments to inward direct investment of a sectoral nature also involve a wide variety of industries, and most frequently those in the service sector, that is, banking, insurance, communications, air transport, international transport and navigation, as well as the natural resources and energy sectors. These controls and obstacles may be such that the access to certain sectors is forbidden or severely restricted. In other cases, limitations are less severe, concerning, for instance, foreign participation in the capital of enterprises, or requirements with respect to the nationality or residence of administrators or directors. Access is sometimes open only when international agreements exist between the country concerned and the country of origin of the investor, or on the basis of reciprocity. Finally, approval of legal establishment is sometimes subject to procedures specific to foreign investors or involving criteria specific to foreign investors.

19. As stated above, access to certain sectors or activities is sometimes forbidden to foreigners or foreign-controlled companies or severely restricted for these. This is the case for banking and broadcasting in Australia; production of war material in Denmark; production and distribution of war material, of explosives for military use, provision of some services for municipalities (open to nationals of other EEC countries) in France; operation of civil aviation in Germany; flour-milling and registration of a fishing vessel in Ireland; agriculture, forestry, fisheries, mining, oil, leather and leather products, broadcasting, airline operations

and coastal shipping in Japan, as well as cable television operations in certain cases; public transport and air transport on a regular schedule in Luxembourg; the film, broadcasting and press sectors and industries related to national defence in Spain; banking in Norway; banking, insurance and broadcasting in Sweden (concessions may be given in certain fields), as well as credit information services and production of war munitions; intra-national air commerce and navigation, production and utilisation of atomic energy, and coastal shipping, dredging or salvaging, radio or tele-communication broadcasting (unless it is found in the public interest for broadcasting) in the United States. Also, a number of States prohibit or limit the ownership of agricultural land by non-resident foreigners or foreign corporations(7).

20. In addition, in Finland, there are some sectors where foreign-owned or -controlled companies are either not permitted at all or where foreign participation is restricted to a certain percentage share, the most common restriction being the maximum 20 per cent participation limit. These sectors are derived from legislation specifically addressing the question of foreign participation or from administrative practice and are as follows: forestry and forest industries, mining, real estate, agriculture, trade in securities, shipping, banking, credit information and auditing firms, estate agencies, printing and publishing, employment agencies, accommodation and catering services, cleaning services, ship brokerage and forwarding, mobile trade, provision of security guards and private detective services and armaments industry. In Greece, special restrictions apply to ownership of Greek vessels, and of capital in banks as well as to maritime transport between Greek ports. In Norway, a ship to be registered as Norwegian has to be owned by Norwegian citizens or companies where Norwegian citizens own at least 60 per cent of the capital and where the majority of the Board, including the Chairman, are Norwegian citizens. Furthermore, acquisition of fishing vessels, fishing with trawlers from Norwegian vessels, air transport within the territory, require concessions which are granted only to Norwegian citizens or companies where Norwegian citizens own a large majority (60 per cent to 66 per cent of the capital) and where all members of the Board are Norwegian citizens. In the Netherlands, the right to fly the Netherlands flag is in general reserved for ships owned by shipowner companies of which two-thirds of the shares are in the possession of Dutch nationals. Similarly, a licence to operate an airline is generally only granted to enterprises which are for the larger part under Dutch control. In New Zealand, non-resident companies other than British Commonwealth companies may not own ships registered in New Zealand. In Switzerland, severe restrictions apply for registration of aircraft and vessels for commercial transportation of goods or people as Swiss aircraft or vessels. Also, the exploration and production of petroleum as well as the construction or exploitation of nuclear energy production units are sometimes submitted to severe restrictions. France has indicated that certain professions are not open to foreigners or to nationals from countries which do not belong to the EEC. This is also the case for one profession in Belgium. Finally, in the United States, there are foreign ownership or citizenship limitations in banking or in operating customs house brokerage(8). Most of these occur at the State level.

21. Several activities cannot be carried out unless concessions or licenses are granted under conditions implying some limitations in foreign participation in the capital of the enterprises or on the board of

_____

7. Severe restrictions also exist for programme companies providing programmes for broadcasting in the United Kingdom. New legislation now before Parliament proposes to amend these restrictions.
8. See paragraph 22 below.

15

administrators or directors of the enterprise concerned. In Australia, proposals by foreign interests involving a non-bank financial intermediary or insurance company should show substantial net economic benefits to Australia to obtain approval. Where these are small, the proposal must show an effective partnership between Australian interests and the foreign investor in the ownership and control of the company concerned. In France, at least two-thirds of the administrators of investment corporations must be nationals of an EEC member country. In Ireland, banks are required to hold a licence, and in order to obtain this licence the following conditions, inter alia, are required to be fulfilled: an applicant for a licence must have paid up a share of not less than Irish £1 million (in the case of non-EEC-owned corporations, an appreciable part of the share capital must be in beneficial Irish ownership): a majority of the Board of Directors shall be Irish nationals or nationals of other members of the EEC; management of day-to-day operations must be in the hands of Irish nationals. Associations or companies with limited liabilities cannot obtain travel agency licences or licences for tour operations unless they are seated in Norway and all members of the Board of Directors are Norwegians. A foreign company of another State carrying on a travel agency or a transport enterprise in their own country can in spite of this obtain a licence from the Ministry of Communications to operate a travel agency in Norway if they satisfy various conditions enumerated in the Act. Enterprises concerned with transport are exempt from the regulations of the law to the extent that they issue tickets to their own routes and/or perform such services which have a natural relation to this issuing of tickets. The exemption does not comprise the arranging of package tours which involve bed-nights, unless the Ministry has given its consent. In Sweden, there are, in principle, nationality requirements for directors and governing board members of limited companies and co-operative societies. However, foreigners are generally, by means of a special permit, allowed to assume such functions. In Switzerland, a company engaged in railroad transport must have a board of administrators including a majority of Swiss citizens residing in Switzerland. Concessions for the construction and exploitation of fuel gas pipelines are not granted to companies significantly controlled by foreign interests. Concessions for the utilisation of water power are only granted to Swiss citizens residing in Switzerland or companies having their headquarters in Switzerland, and at least two-thirds of the board of administrators must be Swiss citizens residing in Switzerland.

22. In the United States, there are certain restrictions on obtaining access to hard mineral deposits on federal lands and obtaining the necessary documentation for vessels to fish in the U.S fishery conservation zone. Also, a foreign-controlled enterprise must meet certain requirements relating to its management in order to obtain a license to operate as a customs broker. Establishment of a bank or opening of a branch or agency by a foreign bank can be effected at the federal or state level. At the state level, this requires approval from the authorities of that state, this approval being sometimes subject to citizenship requirements for management or to reciprocity. Multi-state banking operations for both U.S. and foreign banking organisations are subject to various prohibitions and restrictions under federal law. While U.S. banking organisations have been subject to these restrictions for some time, restrictions on the ability of foreign banks to establish a multi-state deposit-taking branch system were first established by the International Banking Act of 1978. Under that act, a foreign banking organisation, like a domestic bank or bank holding company, must restrict its offices that accept domestic deposits (subsidiaries and/or full service branches) to a single state, except to the extent it has "grandfathered" branches and subsidiary banks outside that state. The 1978 Banking Act provides these banks with the possibility of forming "Edge Act Corporations", allowing them to have a

presence, limited to international banking activities, in several states. As far as insurance is concerned, there are no restrictions at the federal or state levels concerning the establishment or the operations of foreign-owned subsidiaries. Licensing requirements exist for branches of foreign-owned companies, at the state level. There are five areas where admission standards specific to foreign or domestic companies that are not resident in the state concerned exist: ownership limitations, deposit require-ments, license renewals, investment requirements and capital requirements. Also, the activities of foreign branches are limited in many states. In addition non-U.S. insurers may be subject to reciprocity provisions.

23. In several countries, some licences or concessions are necessary to engage in certain activities and are granted to foreign citizens or foreign-controlled enterprises only if there are international treaties involving their countries of origin. In France, this is the case for pub-lishing activities, road transport services and car rental activities, for nationals of countries which do not belong to the EEC. Also, administra-tors of farming co-operative associations must be nationals of an EEC mem-ber country. Air transport within Norwegian territory is reserved for airplanes of Norwegian nationality or nationality of a foreign country when it is based on bilateral air transport agreements with Norway, or special permission from the air transport authorities. Similar conditions apply for air transport in Sweden and Switzerland. In Canada, foreign banks are permitted to incorporate subsidiaries under the 1980 Bank Act, and to commence business on the basis of reciprocal treatment for Canadian banks. Furthermore, the size and growth of the foreign banking sector is limited and there are reserve requirements specific to foreign banks, as well as other limitations on their activities. In the United States, a foreigner or foreign-controlled enterprise may not acquire rights-of-way for oil pipelines or leases or interests therein, for mining coal, oil, or certain other minerals on federal lands, other than the Continental Shelf, if the foreign investor's home country does not permit such mineral leas-ing to U.S.-controlled enterprises(9). In France, certain professions are not open to foreigners or nationals of countries which do not belong to the EEC unless reciprocity agreements exist with those countries.

24. In addition, in many countries there are sector-specific establish-ment requirements for government or regulatory approval which are either specific to foreign investors or involve criteria specific to foreign in-vestors. This is the case for non-bank financial intermediaries, civil aviation, and press activities in Australia; credit institutions and banks in Germany; banks and insurance companies in Italy; retail trade, craft activities, agriculture(10) and insurance in France; fishing in the 200-mile exclusive economic zone or purchasing land which is zoned for rural purposes in New Zealand; shipping transport by foreign vessels in inland waterways, leasing of Swedish vessels to foreign entities, and transport in Sweden; banking and insurance in Switzerland; air transport, and in-surance for companies whose head office is not in a member state of the European Communities in the United Kingdom; radio or television broadcast-ing in Canada, Japan and the United States.

25. In all Member countries there are, of course, many activities subject to concessions or licences or authorisations granted under conditions which apply similarly to domestic and foreign applicants. However, as such, these cannot be considered as obstacles to foreign investment and thus are not covered in the survey.

---

9. Reciprocity provisions also exist a the state level for banking and insurance. See paragraph 22 above.
10. A new law is forthcoming for this particular item.

C. PUBLIC, PRIVATE OR MIXED MONOPOLIES

26. Sectors covered by public, private or mixed monopolies fall under the following main categories in most countries: postal services, telegraph, telephone and telecommunications, broadcasting, transport, energy production and distribution, alcohol production and distribution, tobacco and games.

27. In many countries, including Australia, Belgium, Denmark, Finland, France, Germany, Ireland, Italy, Japan, Luxembourg, Netherlands, New Zealand, Norway, Spain, Sweden, Switzerland and the United Kingdom, a public monopoly, a private monopoly or a mixed monopoly covers the field of postal services, telegraph and telephone services and telecommunications. There are many variations as to the extent of these monopolies. For instance, in Denmark and Luxembourg, the monopoly is restricted to the postal service. In Finland, telecommunications are not covered by a monopoly. In Ireland, the monopoly on postal services does not extend to parcels, and in Switzerland, concessions may be accorded for telecommunications activities which have a purely private purpose. In the United States, the Communications Satellite Corporation was established by the Communications Satellite Act of 1962 as a private corporation to establish and operate a commercial satellite system. Under the Act, not more than an aggregate of 20 per cent of the shares of its stock which are offered to the public may be held by aliens, foreign governments, or foreign-owned, -registered or -controlled corporations. In addition, broadcasting is covered by a public, private or mixed monopoly in Belgium, Finland, France, Germany, Luxembourg, the Netherlands, New Zealand, Norway, Sweden and Switzerland (public broadcasting).

28. As far as transport is concerned, air transport is covered by public, private or mixed monopolies in Australia, Belgium, New Zealand, Switzerland (for certain general interest lines) and Finland (for scheduled civil aviation). In addition, construction and exploitation of airfields and maintenance and exploitation of inland waterways and some harbours are covered by monopolies in Belgium. In these countries, with the exception of Switzerland and the addition of Finland, France, the Netherlands, Norway, Spain and the United Kingdom, monopolies also cover rail services (limited to passenger rail services in Australia). In Switzerland, the right to transportation of passengers on a regular basis belongs to the national post, telephone and telegraph company when this right is not modified by other federal laws (concerning, for instance, railway transport). Concessions can be given to other companies but under various conditions, including the condition that they should not overly compete with public transport companies.

29. In the energy sector, electricity production is covered by public, private or mixed monopolies in Australia, Italy, the Netherlands, New Zealand, France and the United Kingdom. In the latter two countries and in Finland, this monopoly also covers distribution, as well as import and export in France. Water and gas distribution are covered by monopolies in Belgium, Finland, Italy, the Netherlands and the United Kindom. This monopoly also applies to gas production. In Spain there is a mixed monopoly in the petroleum sector. In France, production and distribution of gas - with the exception of natural gas - is under a monopoly, as is the import of energy resources for the production of nuclear energy. Coal production is also under a monopoly in France. In the United Kingdom, privately-owned mines may only operate with a licence from the National Coal Board. In exchange for the licence to carry out mining activities, private mines must pay a royalty to the National Coal Board. Their number of employees and the annual output of private mines is limited by

statute. In Luxembourg and Norway, electricity distribution is covered by public monopolies, as well as import and export of electricity in Norway.

30. In Finland, the manufacture and trade of alcoholic beverages are covered by monopolies. This is also the case for import and sales of alcoholic beverages in Norway, Sweden and Finland (where export is also covered), and for the tobacco industry in Japan, Spain and France (extending to matches). Similarly, in Switzerland the manufacture and import of spirits is handled by a public monopoly. In Australia, effecting lotteries is covered by a monopoly, as in Norway and Sweden for effecting betting on sports events.

31. Finally, the distribution of selected primary products is covered by monopolies in Australia (e.g. wheat, wool and eggs); as is the import/export or distribution of textile fibres relating to fishing, grains, concentrated foods, medicines, drugs and raw fish in Norway; and the import and distribution of salt as well as the import of flour for bakery products in Switzerland. In Japan, the purchase, import, manufacturing and sale of salt are monopolised by the government. In Finland and Sweden, a public monopoly exists in the field of employment services. In Sweden, the retail trade of pharmaceutical products is also covered by a public monopoly. In some German "Länder" and in some Swiss Cantons there exist monopolies in the sector of fire insurance for buildings in favour of the respective public insurance institutions. In one "Land" there exists a monopoly for the insurance of animals for slaughter in favour of a public insurance institution. In Portugal, Law No. 46/77 of 8th July, 1977, lists the many activities restricted to public initiative unless exceptional circumstances are met(11). These include the production and distribution of energy and water resources for public use, many transport and telecommunication activities, the production of war material, many chemical industry activities and steel production. In addition, ownership of natural resources is a State monopoly, and banking activities are restricted to the activities of public banks and three private banks, of which two are foreign. In Spain, a monopoly exists for insurance covering commercial and political risks arising from external trade transactions carried out for the government.

---

11. This Law is in the process of being revised.

Table I

RESTRICTIONS, IMPEDIMENTS, AUTHORISATION PROCEDURES AND OTHER REGULATIONS OF A GENERAL NATURE

Country	Reservation or derogation covering restrictions of a general nature(1)	Authorisation procedures, regulations and impediments of a general nature
AUSTRALIA(2)	Full reservation	Prior authorisation is required for certain investments in Australia by foreign interests irrespective of whether a capital inflow would be involved. Each proposal is considered on its merits to determine whether it is not contrary to the national interest. This examination process requires an assessment to be made of national economic and other benefits and costs. The Government, however, is not normally concerned with the commercial merit of a project - rather this is considered to be a matter for judgement by the parties. The criteria used in this examination process vary depending on the individual case, but in the main, they encompass the net economic benefits including employment opportunities offered by the proposal, the level of Australian equity participation and management involved, and the likely effect of the proposal on the Government's general economic and social policies. Foreign interests should not engage in real estate investment that is of a speculative nature or that is intended purely for capital gain or investment income without accompanying benefits to the Australian economy. In the case of established foreign controlled enterprises, authorisation is required for takeovers and for the creation of new businesses in non-related areas.
AUSTRIA	Limited reservation which applies only to the extent that the authorities of certain provinces have the right to restrict the acquisition of real estate by foreigners or non-residents.	Authorisations for investments by non-residents are granted by the Austrian National Bank. Non-resident investors must prove lasting economic relations with the domestic undertaking involved when applying for an authorisation. Direct investment in the form of loans is only authorised if the project concerned serves to foster productive capacity. No authorisation is required for investment by established foreign-controlled enterprises. The Federal Provinces, under their own constitutionally granted authority, permit the acquisition of real estate by foreigners only subject to approval by the Real Estate Commission, which forms part of the municipal and provincial administration.
BLEU		No authorisation is necessary to carry out a foreign direct investment in Belgium and Luxembourg. Authorisation is required, however, for public take-over bids either by persons not residing in an EEC country or by established non-EEC foreign-controlled enterprises. The only required formality relates to transfers associated with direct investments. The investor must submit a written declaration indicating the purpose of the operation to a bank approved by the Belgium-Luxembourg Exchange Institute. Based upon this declaration, the bank automatically makes the transfer over the free exchange market. If the investor prefers that the transfer take place on the official exchange market, an authorisation from the Exchange Institute is required. This authorisation is not an obstacle to foreign investment but gives the investor the possibility of transferring capital related to financial operations through the official exchange market when the rate on that market is more favourable than on the free market. Such authorisation is practically never refused.
CANADA	Does not adhere to the Code	The Foreign investment Review Act applies to two forms of foreign investments: i) the acquisition of control of an existing Canadian business enterprise by foreign persons; ii) the establishment of a new business in Canada, either by foreign persons who do not already have an existing business in Canada, or by foreign persons in Canada, if the new business is unrelated to the existing business. The Act is concerned with the acquisition of control of a Canadian business enterprise, but not with acquisition of shares where such investment does not involve ultimate control of the business. Under the Act, the Government may allow only those new investments or acquisitions which are, or are likely to be, of significant benefit to Canada. Moreover, foreign investors subject to review under the Act are encouraged to offer commitments to the Canadian Government which define clearly their future intentions. While offering these commitments or undertakings is not mandatory, it can make up an important part of the factors on which a decision to allow an investment is based. The notice requirements and the authorisation procedures of the Act apply to "non-eligible persons" meaning an individual who is neither a Canadian citizen nor a landed immigrant within the meaning of the Immigration Act, a foreign government or political sub-division, a foreign-controlled corporation, or a group containing one or more of the above. Authorisation is not required for "non-eligible persons" who control established businesses in Canada, if they propose to expand their businesses within the confines of "essentially similar products or services" or if they establish new businesses by diversifying into productive activities "related" to their established businesses. Guidelines concerning related businesses were issued on the 18th July, 1975 to set out various modes of relatedness.

1. Reservations or derogations covering only restrictions by sectors are mentioned in Table III below.
2. The only comprehensive and up-to-date statement of Australia's foreign investment policies and procedures which is issued by the responsible Minister, the Treasurer, is contained in the publication, Your Investment in Australia: A Guide for Investors, 1981, pages 7-15, 28-41.

Table I (Cont'd)

Country	Reservation or derogation covering restrictions of a general nature[1]	Authorisation procedures, regulations and impediments of a general nature
DENMARK		Authorisation for inward direct investment is required only if: 1) the total foreign investment in the business enterprise concerned exceeds Kroner 1 million per calendar year, or 2) the investment is made in a business enterprise the object of which exclusively or to any considerable extent is to carry on capital investments abroad or financing of non-residents, or 3) the investment is made by a foreign business enterprise in which a resident directly or indirectly possesses assets representing a direct investment. Long-term financial loans not exceeding Kr. 20 million a year may be raised abroad without permission for the financing of most categories of fixed business investments. In other cases, authorisation is needed but is granted according to a liberal practice when the loan is covered by the OECD definition of a direct investment. No authorisation is required for investment by established foreign-controlled enterprises.
FINLAND		Authorisation of the Bank of Finland to import the direct investment capital is needed and automatically granted provided that the direct investment falls outside the restricted sectors. Establishing a company by non-residents and by foreign-controlled resident enterprises requires prior authorisation of the Government (Act on the right of foreigners and corporations to own real estate and shares in Finland, 28.7.1939). According to the above-mentioned Act permission of the Government is required for foreign or foreign controlled enterprises to purchase or lease real estate for more than two years. Aliens, foreign corporations, established foreign controlled enterprises and Finnish corporations without a foreigners' clause in its articles of association may not acquire non-free shares. Non-free shares are those which by virtue of the restricting clause ("foreigners' clause") in the articles of association of a company limited by shares are tied to Finnish Nationals.
FRANCE		1) Investment from non-EEC Member countries: Prior authorisation of the Ministry of Economics is normally required for this investment, whether it is made by non-residents or by French companies under foreign control. The following operations, however, do not require prior authorisation provided they are financed by means of foreign currency: - up to Frs.5 million per calendar year: new investment in French enterprises by non-residents who have already been authorised to participate in them, provided that the new operation does not increase the percentage of their participation; - up to Frs.5 million per calendar year: purchasing or setting up handicraft or retail trade enterprises to be operated by the non-resident investor himself; - without any limitation: setting up of real estate enterprises. 2) Investment from EEC Member countries: Investment from EEC Member countries are subject only to prior notification except in the following cases: - investment by enterprises controlled by residents of non-EEC Member countries; - investment in sectors of activity which participate in France, even only occasionally, in the administration of public authority; - investment affecting public order, health or security as well as investment in activities related to the production of or trading in weapons, ammunition and war material; - operations the effect of which would be to obstruct the application of French laws and regulations. Operations which do not conform to the required conditions are subject to the authorisation regime described under (1) above; the Minister for Economics must notify non-compliance with the required conditions within two months of the receipt of the corresponding declaration. Operations subject to declaration must be financed in accordance with the general provisions of exchange control, i.e. by means of foreign currency contributions; borrowings between France and abroad (other than loans over five years maturity which constitute a direct investment) are subject to the authorisation regime described under (1) above. Most operations are only subject to foreign currency financing conditions; these conditions are liberal in the case of the establishment of new companies and more severe in the case of the purchase or participation in an existing company (foreign currency financing is normally required in this case). However, in some exceptional cases of investment from non-EEC Member countries, the authorities use their control powers to control whether "in view of the amount involved or of other factors a specific transaction or transfer would

1. Reservations or derogations covering only restrictions by sectors are mentioned in Table III below.

Table I (Cont'd)

Country	Reservation of derogation covering restrictions of a general nature(1)	Authorisation procedures, regulations and impediments of a general nature
FRANCE (Cont'd)		have an exceptionally detrimental effect on the interests" of France, which is one of the restrictions on liberalisation stipulated by the Capital Movements Code. Certain authorisations are, in effect, conditional on the results which relate especially to the maintenance or the creation of jobs, regional development or exports. The authorities of course monitor the fulfilment of the agreements thus taken.
GERMANY		No authorisation is needed.
GREECE		The importation of capital from abroad is not subject to authorisation in Greece. However, if the investor wishes to repatriate the imported capital, to remit abroad part of the profits earned and/or interest payable on such capital and to enjoy secure property rights, guarantees against unilateral actions, and repatriation guarantees up to fixed percentages, (with other possible benefits including exemptions from duties and preferential tax treatment), he may, if he so desires, request that the proposed investment should be deemed "productive" under the provision of Law Decree 2687/1953 re: "investment and protection of foreign capital" which is guaranteed by a special dispensation of the Greek Constitution. Direct investors who have not applied for benefits under the above law, must submit an application to the Currency Committee of the Bank of Greece, which examines the advisibility of these investment proposals in order to ensure the repatriation of interest, profits and capital. Foreign investments involving the acquisition of real estate in border regions may be restricted.
IRELAND		Non-residents of Ireland wishing to make a direct investment in the state are required to obtrain exchange control approval. Investment by enterprises already established in Ireland which are foreign-controlled does not require permission.
ITALY		Foreign direct investment does not require authorisation. Two procedures may be followed in carrying out investment operations. The first is purely administrative and the second is provided under Act No. 43 of 7th February, 1956. Under the administrative procedure foreign investors may at present have inward transfers of funds credited to "capital accounts", and may transfer abroad, through these same accounts, profits and proceeds of sale of investments. The authenticity of these operations must of course be verified by the bank acting as intermediary. The second procedure, provided under the aforementioned Act, distinguishes between investments defined as productive (Section 1 of the Act) and other investments (Section 2). For both categories, foreign investors have the benefit of a guarantee of transferability of profits and of the proceeds of any sale of investment, but this guarantee, while being without limit in the first case, is subject to certain restrictions in the second. The investment must be recognised by the Ministry of the Treasury, as productive. Failure to observe the conditions laid down for entitlement to this procedure does not void the operation, but the advantages provided under the Act are forfeited. However, for outward transfers which cannot be made under the Act, the foreign investor may also avail himself of the administrative procedure using the "capital accounts" mentioned earlier.
JAPAN		Under the amended Foreign Exchange Law, implemented on 1st December, 1980, foreign direct investors are required to make a prior notification before proceeding with the investments. These are automatically approved except in the four excepted industries and subject to safeguard clauses where the Minister of Finance and the other competent Minister(s) deem Japanese interests to be adversely affected.
NETHERLANDS		Inward direct investment in the form of capital participation is not subject to authorisation. Loans from non-resident parent companies are subject to license from the Netherlands Bank which will be given in the case of long-term loans, e.g. with a fixed maturity of 5 years or more. Foreign controlled domestic enterprises, once established, are considered resident for the purpose of exchange control regulations (which concern transactions between residents and non-residents only). Acquisitions (whether by residents or by non-residents) by way of a public offer are subject to certain rules established in a code by the Social Economic Council (SER). These rules seek to protect the interests of the shareholders and are aimed at the correct pricing of the shares. Mergers and acquisitions are subject to rules in this code to give the trade unions concerned the opportunity to express in due time their advisory opinion of the merger from the point of view of the employees. The same code prescribes notification of proposed mergers with the government.
NEW ZEALAND	Full reservation	All inward direct investment requires authorisation by the Overseas Investment Commission. Consent is required where a takeover would give a non-resident control of 25 per cent or more of any class of share in New Zealand incorporated enterprises. Applications are examined on a case by case basis taking into account the benefits to New Zealand. These regulations also apply to the continuing operation of foreign companies once established. Consent is required for any subsequent takeover of 25 per

Table I (Cont'd)

Country	Reservation of derogation covering restrictions of a general nature(1)	Authorisation procedures, regulations and impediments of a general nature
NEW ZEALAND (Cont'd)		Purely portfolio investment is limited to 24.9 per cent while all other cases are treated on their merits.
NORWAY		Direct investments from abroad are subject to individual authorisation by the Norges Bank. The same authorisation procedure applies to increases of existing direct investments as to new investments. According to the Act of 14th December, 1917, relating to Acquisitions of waterfalls, mines and other real properties, foreigners and Norwegian companies with foreign property interests will need a concession for purchases of real property, whether building and/or land, and without regard to the purpose for which the property will be used. Leases of real property for a period of more than ten years are also subject to a concession. If the property is to be used for industrial purposes or refining of fish, a concession is required without regard to the lease period. A foreign controlled company is defined as a company where more than 20 per cent of the voting rights or the share capital is owned by foreigners or foreign controlled companies or where at least one member of the board is an alien. Foreigners and foreign-controlled companies must have a concession to acquire more than 10 per cent of the share capital of a company owning or leasing real property subject to concession. According to the 1917 Act a concession can be granted unless it would be contrary to the public interest. The concession terms are stipulated in each case by the Ministry of Industry. It is thus usually required that the chairman and the majority of the board of directors are Norwegian citizens, and that transactions between the Norwegian subsidiary and its foreign parent company are based upon realistic pricing and optimum conditions for the Norwegian company. Agreements between subsidiary and parent firms regarding payments for economic, technical, mercantile and other assistance must also be approved by the Norwegian authorities. The conditions may also regulate the type of production, financing terms and other circumstances, varying from company to company. Pursuant to the Joint-Stock Companies Act of 4th June, 1976, the manager in a joint-stock company, at least half of the members of the board of directors, the corporate assembly and the committee of representatives, must be permanently resident in Norway, i.e. they must reside there and have resided there for the last two years. The rules are applied irrespective of the lines of business. The Ministry of Commerce and Shipping may in exceptional cases grant exemptions from these rules. Under the Norwegian concession laws, only companies having their seat in Norway and an executive board where the majority of the members, including the chairman are Norwegian citizens, may obtain a concession to purchase electric power in larger quantities than 1000 kw. Moreover, in the case of companies having foreigners on their executive board or whose basic capital is not entirely domestically-owned, the State may, in the concession terms, reserve a right to purchase, not later than 40 years from the concession date, the factory plants established for the purpose of utilising the power, together with land, buildings, machinery, facilities, etc.
PORTUGAL	Limited reservation which applies only: a) to foreign participation beyond specified limits in the capital of enterprises belonging to certain sectors of the economy which are governed by special legislation; and b) to cases where the authorities consider that the capital to be imported would not be used in ventures likely to be of interest in the economic development of the country.	Foreign direct investment in Portugal is subject to a case-by-case authorisation procedure. The Foreign Investment Code (Decree-Law No. 348/77) specifies two forms of authorisation: the general form, applicable to most proposals; the contractual form, reserved to projects which by their size or other characteristics are of particular interest to the national economy. Under the contractual form, special benefits can be granted to authorised investments. Authorisation is automatically granted (i) for capital increases of existing enterprises with foreign participation (if the percentage of foreign control remains unchanged and provided that the regulations or initial authorisation permit); (ii) for investments not exceeding Esc.5 million annually with a view towards strengthening an existing enterprise with foreign participation (providing that the level of non-resident participation remains the same) and (iii) for investment in priority sectors defined by a resolution of the Council of Ministers (provided that the conditions established by the resolution are observed). Prior authorisation is required for extension of activities of established foreign controlled enterprises into new fields.
SPAIN	Limited reservation on investment in the form of long-term loans which does not apply to loans in the form of purchases or of subscriptions to bonds, nor where there is a parent company/subsidiary company relationship between the lender and the borrower.	Notification is required in all cases, for statistical purposes. As a general rule, foreign investments in Spanish firms are free up to 50 per cent of their capital. Above 50 per cent the investor has to apply for an authorisation which is granted in almost all cases. In the last two years, 96 per cent - as an average - of the total value of all applications submitted for authorisation has been granted. No administrative authorisation for majority investments is required for investments in certain sectors (oil research and exploitation, industrial equipment industries), nor for investments in companies, branch offices and commercial establishments with equity up to 25 million pts. and for investment in real estate also up to 25 millions pts. Investments by foreign controlled enterprises are subject to the same rules. However no authorisation is needed for increases in equity which do not alter the foreign controlled percentage of the firm, made from freely disposable reserves or when such increases are due to normal company growth.

1. Reservations or derogations covering only restrictions by sectors are mentioned in Table III below.

Table I (Cont'd)

Country	Reservation of derogation covering restrictions of a general nature(1)	Authorisation procedures, regulations and impediments of a general nature
SWEDEN		Direct investment in fields covered by the National Resources Law of 1916 can only be made with the permission of the Government. Exchange control authorisation by the Sveriges Riksbank is also needed. Applications, which as a rule are made through resident agents or partners of the investor, must give particulars of the latter's activities abroad and of his plans in Sweden. They may be brief and informal and are speedily dealt with. Borrowing in Sweden by residents (including foreign controlled enterprises) against guarantee of non-residents (including parent companies) require permission by the Sveriges Riksbank. **Acquisition of non-free (tied) shared** Aliens, foreign corporations, established foreign controlled enterprises and Swedish corporations without a foreigners' clause in its Articles of Association may not acquire non-free shares. Non-free shares are those which by virtue of the restricting clause ("foreigners' clause") in the Articles of Association of a company limited by shares are tied to Swedish nationals. A provision on tied shares has its main bearing on the acquisition of real property. In order to close the possibility for an alien or a foreign corporation to acquire real property by acquiring instead the shares of a Swedish company which owns real property the following rules are applicable: A Swedish company is allowed freely to acquire real property and in this context avoid classification as a foreign corporation only by including a foreigners' clause in its Articles of Association, whereby less than 20 per cent of voting rights and 40 per cent of the share capital can be acquired by a foreigner (or by a Swedish company which is without a foreigners' clause in its Articles of Association i.e. the limits above are exceeded according to the company's articles). In order to allow a more extensive foreign control over Swedish limited companies a foreigners' clause in the articles must be removed. It calls for a special permit which in practice is liberally granted. **Acquisition of real property** Aliens and foreign corporations must have a special permit to acquire real property (including hydro-power and transformation of power). Such permit is generally granted where the property is needed for the activities of the enterprise. Also the right to claim mineral deposits, to acquire or work claimed minerals or engage in mining requires a special permit. In the case of residential and office buildings, building sites, et., permission is given by country authorities. **Acquisition of shares in trading partnerships** Aliens, foreign corporations and Swedish limited companies without a foreigners' clause in their Articles of Association may not, without a special permit, take part in such partnerships.
SWITZERLAND		No authorisation required for investment by non-residents or by established foreign-controlled enterprises. The acquisition of real estate in Switzerland is subject to authorisations from the competent Cantonal authorities when the real estate is purchased by physical persons domiciled abroad or resident in Switzerland for less than five years (with the exception of physical persons entitled to establish themselves in Switzerland), or by legal persons whose head office either is not in Switzerland or is in Switzerland but the financing of which depends for a major part on the participation of persons not having their domicile or their head office in Switzerland. Authorisation must be granted where the buyer has a legitimate interest in the acquisition, for instance where the real estate concerned is to be used wholly or to a great extent as the permanent premises of an undertaking engaged in trade, operating a factory or carrying on any other form of commercial business. (Federal Arrêté on the acquisition of real estate by persons domiciled abroad). The Board of joint stock companies (with the exception of holding companies) must include a majority of persons residing in Switzerland and of Swiss nationality.
UNITED KINGDOM		No authorisation required for investment by non-residents or by established foreign-controlled enterprises. The Industry Act of 1975 gives the Government the powers necessary to prohibit a proposed transfer of control of an important United Kingdom manufacturing undertaking to a non-resident where the transfer is considered contrary to the interests of the United Kingdom or a significant part of it. If it is considered that the national interest cannot appropriately be protected in any other way, property in such a proposal or completed transfer may be compulsorily acquired against compensation. Both prohibition and vesting orders are subject to Parliamentary approval. These powers have not been used hereto; they may be used for reasons of essential security interests as for other purposes.
UNITED STATES		No authorisation required for investment by non-residents or by established foreign-controlled enterprises. Some states prohibit or limit the ownership of land by non-resident foreigners or foreign corporations.

1. Reservations or derogations covering only restrictions by sectors are mentioned in Table III below.

Table II

RESTRICTIONS ON LOCAL FINANCING OF INWARD DIRECT INVESTMENT: REGULATIONS
ON ACCESS TO THE DOMESTIC CAPITAL MARKET BY NON-RESIDENT INVESTORS

Country	Funds raised by the non-resident investor for the creation of a new enterprise, a joint venture, participation in or take over of an existing enterprise	
	Share issues, bond issues or other long-term borrowing	Short-term borrowing
AUSTRALIA	Non-residents proposing to invest in Australia are not permitted to raise funds locally. However, once a non-resident investor has established an enterprise in Australia, such an enterprise is a resident for exchange control purposes and may raise funds locally; although those proposing to borrow locally are encouraged to raise their funds through increasing local equity by means of new share issues or other placements.	
AUSTRIA	i) By share issues or bond issues; each case is decided on its own merits ii) By long-term borrowing: authorisation is given upon application by the Bank of Austria	Authorisation is given upon application by the Bank of Austria
BELGIUM	Same treatment applied to non residents and to residents as regards shares and debt securities other than bonds. On the other hand, the introduction of foreign bonds and the issue through placing or public sale of foreign bonds on the Belgian capital market are subject to authorisation.	Same treatment applied to non-residents and to residents
CANADA	Same treatment applied to non-residents and to residents	
DENMARK	Restrictions are applied to issues of shares and bonds by non-residents on the domestic capital market. Long-term financial loans may not be granted to non-residents without permission from Danmarks Nationalbank. Practice is restrictive for substantial amounts. For the financing of direct investments no fixed proportions are applied with respect to funds to be brought in from abroad and funds being raised on the domestic capital market by the foreign-controlled resident enterprise itself.	Short-term financial loans may not be granted to non-residents without permission from Danmarks Nationalbank. Practice is restrictive for substantial amounts.
FINLAND	Non-resident share issues and long-term borrowing (for amounts exceeding F.Mk.50,000) require an authorisation by the Bank of Finland. In case of bond issues, same procedure as for resident investors: authorisation by the Council of State. For balance-of-payments reasons a restrictive attitude is maintained in regulating these operations. Initial investment is usually totally financed from abroad.	Restrictively controlled by the Bank of Finland for amounts exceeding F.Mk.50,000.
FRANCE	For initial establishment: Authorisation subject to the financing conditions which had been granted depending upon the balance-of-payments situation. For participations or take overs: Capital import is generally required.	
GERMANY	Same treatment applied to non residents and to residents	
GREECE	No information is available	
IRELAND	Restrictions are applied to the issue of shares and bonds in local currency by non-residents on the domestic capital markets. Non-residents require the prior approval of the Central Bank of Ireland to borrow funds locally for inward direct investment. Normally investors located outside the EEC must finance fixed assets with funds introduced from abroad. They are normally allowed to borrow working capital locally. EEC investors are permitted to finance entire inward direct investments through local borrowing.	
ITALY	Placing of shares and bonds in Italy by non-residents (not carrying on business in Italy through firms owned by them and established and and operating in Italy) and long-term loans contracted in Italy by non-residents for the purpose of subsequent direct investment, are governed by the provisions in the Exchange Control Regulations on the purchase of foreign shares by residents and on the granting of loans, regardless of the destination of the funds. In particular, the purchase of unquoted foreign shares and bonds by residents, and the placing of bonds and contracting of loans by non-residents, require authorisation, since both cases involve Italian financing abroad.	Subject to authorisation by the Ministry of Foreign Trade, except for short-term borrowing in favour of residents in EEC countries, within certain conditions and limits of amounts.
JAPAN	Same treatment applied to non-residents and to residents	
LUXEMBOURG	Same treatment applied to non-residents and to residents	
NETHERLANDS	Share issues by non-residents are free of licence. Bond issues require a licence from the Netherlands Bank which will be given subject to the issues calendar if larger than Fl.16 million. Borrowing for longer than 2 years from domestic banks and non-banks (e.g. institutional investors) is free up to Fl.10 million a year per borrower. Over Fl.10 million a licence is needed, which will be given subject to possible scheduling. The proceeds are allowed to be made available to resident subsidiaries in the form of share capital or in the form of long-term loans e.g. with fixed maturity of 5 years or more.	Borrowing by non-residents for less than 2 years is free. However, the proceeds are not allowed to be made available to resident subsidiaries on a short-term basis (see column 2).
NEW ZEALAND	Prior authorisation is required	
NORWAY	Prior authorisation is required	

25

Table II (Cont'd)

Country	Funds raised by the non-resident investor for the creation of new enterprise, a joint venture, participation in or take over of an existing enterprise	
	Share issues, bond issues or other long-term borrowing	Short-term borrowing
PORTUGAL	Same treatment to non-resident and to resident investors as regards access to medium-term financing if foreign participation does not exceed 25 per cent of the corresponding capital: - if the participation is between 25 and 50 per cent local financing permitted up to 70 per cent of paid-up equity and reserves less any accumulated losses; - if the foreign participation is more than 50 per cent, local financing permitted up to 50 per cent of paid-up equity and reserves less any accumulated losses.	
SPAIN	Access to the domestic credit market (including the discount of paper, bond issues, fixed interest securities and all types of loans) is subject to the following regulations: a) if the foreign participation does not exceed 25 per cent of the registered capital of a Spanish enterprise to be created, or already created, or whose registered capital is to be increased, in the last two cases the enterprise, and in the first case the "non-resident investor", may borrow on the medium and long-term domestic market, using any loan-raising instrument, on the same terms as a Spanish enterprise having no foreign capital participation. b) if the foreign participation exceeds 25 per cent of the registered capital the enterprise or investor is allowed to borrow on the domestic market up to five times the amount of the shareholders' funds (equity and operational reserves). c) for certain financial companies the limit established in (b) can be raised to thirteen times the shareholders' funds. Local financing can be obtained beyond these limits with the authorisation of the Directorate General of Financial Policy. Complementary regulations establish certain exceptions to the general rule and clarifications, mainly: 1. No authorisation is required for access to domestic credit beyond these limits: a) if the enterprise obtains foreign financing in a proportion comparable to that existing between the national and foreign ownership and with similar maturities; b) for investment in industrial equipment; c) for investment to finance exports. 2. The credits of a participating nature granted by the parent company or foreign investor will be considered as shareholders funds.	Same rules apply to short-term borrowing. In general, short-term borrowing (not exceeding 18 months) is allowed for creating Spanish enterprises with participation of foreign capital.
SWEDEN	Prior authorisation required. Normally one-half of the investment in fixed assets must be financed with transfers from the parent company abroad, except where the amounts are below Kr.5 million.	Normally permitted
SWITZERLAND	All banks or financial institutions subject to Article 8 of the law on banks and saving banks must obtain an authorisation from the Swiss national bank before carrying out the following operations in favour of non-residents: - issue of bonds - issue of shares - granting of credits - placing of medium term debt certificates ("notes") An authorisation is necessary insofar as the maturity of the operation is at least equal to 1 year and the amount is at least equal to Sw.Frs.10 million (3 million for notes).	Loans of less than one year duration that banks and financial institutions grant to non-residents are not subject to any limitation. But non-residents are not allowed to issue securities on the Swiss money market.
UNITED KINGDOM	Same treatment applied to non-residents and to residents	
UNITED STATES	Same treatment applied to non-residents and to residents.	

Table III
SECTORAL CONTROLS AND OBSTACLES TO INWARD DIRECT INVESTMENT

Country	Reservations or derogations covering only restrictions by sectors	Sectors where obstacles apply specifically or more severely to non-resident investors	Sectors closed to foreign investment due to public or privately operated (or mixed) monopolies
AUSTRALIA(1)		**Banking** Foreigners not granted authority to carry on banking business in Australia or to acquire interests in existing Australian banks. **Non-bank financial intermediaries and insurance companies** Proposals by foreign interests involving a non-bank financial intermediary or insurance company should show substantial net economic benefits to Australia to obtain approval. Where these are small, the proposal must involve an effective partnership between Australian interests and the foreign investor in the ownership and control of the company concerned. The implications of the proposal for the financial sector and the level of Australian management and control following the proposals implementation are also taken into consideration. **Newspapers** All proposals for foreign investment in newspapers in Australia are subject to case-by-case assessment. Foreign investment in mass circulation newspapers is restricted. Further, approval is not normally given to proposals by foreign interests to invest in ethnic newspapers in Australia, unless there is substantial involvement by the local ethnic community and effective local control of editorial policy. **Broadcasting and television** No less than 80 per cent of the issued share capital of a broadcasting or T.V. company must be owned by Australian residents. No single overseas shareholder may have more than 15 per cent of the issued capital of such a company. **Civil aviation** Foreign equity in domestic airlines is restricted. For general aviation, all foreign investment proposals subject to case-by-case assessment.	**Public monopolies** - international aviation - postal services - telephone and telegraph services - international communication - passenger rail services - electricity production - water distribution - distribution of selected primary products (e.g. wheat, wool, and eggs. **Privately-operated or mixed monopolies** - domestic commercial aviation - lotteries - gas distribution
AUSTRIA(1)		Defence	Information not available
BELGIUM		Foreigners not allowed to be exchange dealers.	**Public monopolies** - air transport (SABENA) - national railways - construction and operation of airports - telephone, telegraph and postal services - inland waterways and ports - radio and television broadcasting - water distribution **Privately-operated monopolies** - local railways and public transport - distribution of gas
CANADA	Does not adhere to the Code	Approval required at Federal level for foreign investment in: - Broadcasting - Mining in Northwest Territories - Oil and gas Foreign banks are permitted to incorporate subsidiaries under the 1980 Bank Act, and to commence business in Canada on the basis of reciprocal treatment for Canadian Banks. A licence is required, and approval of the Minister of Finance necessary for a foreign bank subsidiary to open branches. The size and growth of the foreign bank sector is limited. Furthermore, there are reserve requirements specific to foreign banks, specific conditions applying to their licencing activities, and limitations on the non-resident or foreign ownership of domestic banks.	

1. Reservations and derogations covering restrictions of a general nature are mentioned in Table I above.

Table III (Cont'd)

Country	Reservations or derogations covering only restrictions by sectors	Sectors where obstacles apply specifically or more severely to non-resident investors	Sectors closed to foreign investment due to public or privately operated (or mixed) monopolies
DENMARK		Permission for production of war material granted only to nationals and to domestic corporations owned by nationals. Sectors regulated by concession laws: transport by rail and bus by privately-owned companies; civil domestic aviation; production and distribution of electricity and gas; extraction and distribution of natural gas and water; extraction of minerals.	Public monopolies - post service - radio and television broadcasting Privately operated monopolies None
FINLAND	Limited reservation which applies "only to the extent that there are limitations on the right of foreigners to engage in certain activities or to acquire, own, lease, or otherwise benefit from certain types of property."	Foreign-owned or controlled companies not permitted - or allowed a limited participation only - in the following sectors: Forestry and forest industries, mining, real estate, agriculture, trade in securities, shipping, banking, credit information and auditing firms, estate agencies, printing and publishing, employment agencies, accommodation and catering services, cleaning services, ship brokerage and forwarding, mobile trade, provision of security guards and private detective services and armaments industry.	Public monopolies - telegraph, telephone and postal services - television and radio broadcasting - export, import and distribution of alcoholic beverages - employment services (labour exchange) - rail transport services - football pools, state lotteries with money prizes and totalizer
FRANCE		**Transport** Activities in the area of road transport and renting of vehicles cannot be carried out by foreigners except in the case of EEC nationals and on the basis of reciprocity. There are exceptions to these rules. **Agriculture** Foreigners - except EEC nationals - must obtain an authorisation in order to run an agricultural concern. The legal regime of agricultural co-operation provides that administrators selected among members of co-operatives must be French, EEC nationals or nationals of a country with which a reciprocal agreement has been concluded. **Insurance** Enterprises with head offices in foreign countries must obtain a licence to operate in France. The licence is granted only for branches of insurance operated by the enterprise concerned in its country of origin. Such enterprises must appoint a general agent who will be responsible for the enterprise in France. A deposit may be required if the country of the head-office requires one from French firms. In the case of enterprises whose head-office is in an EEC country, a licence for insurance other than life can only be refused for administrative reasons (mostly solvency of the head-office) and no licence is required for re-insurance. The provisions concerning freedom of establishment of life assurance enterprises within the EEC are not applicable yet in France but will be so in the near future. Brokers in the field of insurance must be French or EEC nationals or nationals of a country which grants reciprocity to France. **Other Regulated Activities** Activities in the following regulated sectors can be carried out by French or EEC nationals or nationals of other countries on a reciprocal basis: - banking and finance - lawyers, notaries, legal advisors and other legal activities - auditors - exchange dealers (agents de change) (French and EEC nationals only) **Manufacture of weapons and trading** Reserved for French nationals **Setting up of a casino** Is subject to authorisation. Managers and employees must be French or EEC nationals.	Public monopolies - explosives - tobacco and matches - television - telephone, telegraph and postal services - public services by municipalities - fuel, coal etc. - electricity and gas - atomic energy - railways

Table III (Cont'd)

Country	Reservations or derogations covering only restrictions by sectors	Sectors where obstacles apply specifically or more severely to non-resident investors	Sectors closed to foreign-investment due to public or privately operated operated (or mixed) monopolies
FRANCE (Cont'd)		**Publishing** The law provides that foreigners may hold shares or participate in the financing of publications issued in France only on the basis of reciprocity.	
GERMANY		**Banking** The setting-up of branch offices of foreign banks requires authorisation (notification only in the case of national credit institutions). The purpose of this requirement is to prevent foreign banks from circumventing legal standards for the protection of potential clients by setting up branch offices instead of domestic subsidiaries. **Aviation** There are moreover limitations to the possibility for non-residents to invest in German civil aviation.	<u>Public monopolies</u> - Organisation for the conveyance of communication items except newspapers & magazines - Telephone & telegraph services (with restricted possibilities for private users) - Radio & television broadcasting In addition, monopolies exist in certain Länder in the sectors of fire-insurance for buildings and, in one case insurance of animals for slaughter.
GREECE		Concession required for mining and mineral rights. Special restrictions apply to ownership of Greek vessels and of capital in banks and to maritime transport between Greek ports.	Information not available
IRELAND	Limited reservation which applies to flour milling, in which foreign ownership is governed by the provisions of the Agricultural Produce (Cereals) Act, 1933.	Fishing vessels, to be eligible for registration, must be owned by an Irish citizen or Irish company. The following requirements (among others which do not involve any discrimination between nationals and foreigners) must be met by banks in order to obtain a licence to operate: - share capital of not less than 1 million must be paid up and, in the case of non-EEC owned corporations, an appreciable part of the share capital must be in beneficial Irish ownership; - a majority of the Board of Directors must be Irish or nationals of other member States of the EEC; - management of day-to-day operations must be in the hands of Irish residents	<u>Public monopolies</u> The Minister for Posts and Telegraphs has a public monopoly (subject to certain defined exeptions) over the collection and delivery of letters, but a similar exclusive privilege does not apply in respect of parcels. The Minister also possesses the exclusive privilege of providing telecommunications (with exceptions).
ITALY		<u>Ownership of ships</u> Foreign nationals and companies may participate in the ownership of Italian ships to an extent not exceeding 12 of the 24 shares; exceptions may be made for companies having a preponderance of Italian interest, whether established in Italy or abroad. <u>Ownership of aircraft</u> The right to own Italian aircraft is reserved to the State, provinces, communes or other Italian public entities; to Italian nationals; to companies formed and having their registered office in Italy, whose capital is two-third owned by Italian nationals and whose Chairman and two-thirds of whose Directors as well as the General Manager are Italian nationals. <u>Operation of a regular air transport service</u> The right to operate an air transport service can only be granted to such persons, companies or institutions as are entitled to own Italian aircraft. However, with regard to international airline services, the right to operate such services may also be granted to foreigners where this is provided for in international conventions.	- Telephone, telegraph and postal services - Electricity, gas, water and nuclear energy - Roads and motorways - Rail transport - Public services by municipalities - Loto and similar games - R.A.1. television broadcasts

Table III (Cont'd)

Country	Reservations or derogations covering only restrictions by sectors	Sectors where obstacles apply specifically or more severely to non-resident investors	Sectors closed to foreign investment due to public or privately operated (or mixed) monopolies
ITALY (Cont'd)		**Establishment of headquarters or branches of foreign banks** The establishment of headquarters or branches of foreign banks requires authorisation issued by order of the Ministry of Finance in consultation with the Ministry for Foreign Affairs, after reference to the Inter-ministerial Committee for Credit and Savings. However, the same procedure applies to branches of banks having their headquarters in other EEC countries as to Italian credit institutions. **Insurance** Italian and foreign insurers must have a licence from the Ministry of Industry to operate in Italy, for all branches of insurance. For insurers from non-EEC countries, the principle of reciprocity applies.	
JAPAN	Limited reservation which only applies to investment in four excepted industries (primary industry related to agriculture, forestry and fisheries, mining, oil and leather and leather products manufacturing)	Licence not given to foreigners, foreign-owned or controlled enterprises in the sectors of broadcasting and airlines and may not be given in the sector of cable television. For coastal shipping, licences given only to Japanese ships.	**Public monopolies** - postal services - tobacco industry - telecommunications (domestic service) - purchase, import, manufacturing and sale of salt **Privately-operated monopoly** - telecommunications (international service)
LUXEMBOURG		- Public transport - Air transport on a regular schedule	- radio and television broadcasting - postal services - electricity distribution.
NETHERLANDS		**Shipping** The right to fly the Netherlands flag is in general reserved for ships owned by Dutch nationals or shipping companies of which two-thirds of the shares are in the possession of Dutch nationals residing in the Netherlands. **Aviation** A licence to operate an airline is generally only granted to enterprises which are for the larger part under Dutch control and under Dutch management. **Banking** Approval of the Netherlands Bank and the Minister of Finance is required for each participation in a domestic commercial bank exceeding five per cent of the share capital. Without this approval the share holder is not allowed to exercise his voting-right. **Indemnity insurance** Branches or subsidiaries of foreign indemnity insurers must obtain a licence to operate in the Netherlands. These licences are granted virtually on the same terms and conditions as to domestic insurers. An additional requirement is the appointment of a representative, resident in the Netherlands. For indemnity insurers with a head office outside the EEC, the rules in respect of the solvency margin, the location of the assets representing this margin and the technical reserves differ from the co-ordinated rules for EEC-insurers. **Life assurance** All foreign life assurers must obtain a licence to operate in the Netherlands. In addition they have to appoint a representative, resident in the Netherlands. Furthermore, they are obliged to give a security of Fl.100.000 and to deposit the assets representing the technical reserves. However, after having adapted the Netherlands legislation to the EEC-life-assurance directive, virtually the same rules as stated above for indemnity insurers will apply to foreign life assurers.	**Public monopolies** - telecommunications and postal services (PTT) - railways (NS) - regional electricity companies - distribution of gas and water **Privately operated or mixed monopolies** - broadcasting - public bus transport

Table III (Cont'd)

Country	Reservations or derogations covering only restrictions by sectors	Sectors where obstacles apply specifically or more severely to non-resident investors	Sectors closed to foreign investment due to public or privately operated (or mixed) monopolies
NEW ZEALAND(1)		**Fishing** A 200 mile exclusive economic zone was introduced in April 1978. Overseas companies can operate within this zone subject to fishing agreements between New Zealand and the foreign government concerned. They may also become partners in approved joint ventures with New Zealand companies to gain access to the zone.	**Public monopolies** - post and telegraph - railways - electricity generation - television stations **Mixed monopolies** - air transport - radio stations
NORWAY	Limited reservation which applies to the transaction only and only to the extent to which there are limitations on the right of non-residents to engage in certain activities or to acquire, own or lease certain types of property.	Ships to be registered as Norwegian must be owned by Norwegian citizens, by a limited partnership where Norwegian citizens own at least 60 per cent of the capital, or by a joint stock company seated in Norway where the majority of the members of the board, including the chairman, are Norwegian citizens living in Norway and where Norwegian citizens own at least 60 per cent of the capital. In exceptional cases, exemptions from the 60 per cent rule are granted. Concession to acquire fishing vessels or shares in a company which owns such vessels is only granted to Norwegian nationals or joint-stock companies seated in Norway, where all members of the board are shareholders and Norwegian nationals with residence in Norway, and further that at least 60 per cent of the equity capital is owned by Norwegian nationals. Fishing with trawls from Norwegian vessels is reserved for Norwegian nationals and the type of company mentioned above. Air transport within Norwegian territory is reserved for air planes of Norwegian nationality except where bilateral air transport agreements with Norway exist, or special permission from the air transport authorities is granted. Concession to operate is only given to Norwegian citizens or to limited liability companies having their registered office in Norway and an entirely Norwegian board of directors and in which at least two-thirds of the capital is Norwegian. The King may in exceptional cases permit a foreign-owned air plane to be registered in Norway. Associations or companies with limited liabilities may obtain travel agency licences and licences for tour operations only if they are seated in Norway and all members of the board of directors are Norwegians. There are however exceptions under specified conditions. A concession is necessary for the establishment of banks. In order to be authorised, a bank must be owned by Norwegian citizens having their residence in Norway. In this connection may be considered as Norwegians: joint-stock companies and other companies with limited liabilities seated in Norway where all the members of the board are Norwegians, and at least two thirds of the basic capital must belong to the State, Norwegian municipalities or Norwegian citizens. The manager in a joint-stock company, irrespective of the line of business, at least half the members of the board of directors, the corporate assembly and the committee of representatives, must be permanent residents in Norway, i.e. they must reside there and have resided there for the last two years. In exceptional cases exemptions from these rules may be granted. Foreign insurance companies are entitled to engage in insurance activities in Norway through a representative and on terms stipulated in the Act relating to insurance companies.	**Public monopolies** - Telephone, telegraph and postal services - Railways - Electricity distribution - Import and sales of alcoholic beverages (sales and retailing subject to licence from the local authorities) - Import of all types of textile fibres and products thereof which are to be used as fishing gear or for producing fishing gear - Import of cereals and concentrated foods - Sale to chemists of medecines, drugs preparations etc. to be used in the production of medecines; import and export of medecines (with exemptions) - Broadcasting - Lotteries with money prizes and betting on sports events **Privately-operated monopolies** - First-hand sales of the predominant part of the catch landing in Norway - Sales of fish and fishery products to foreign markets

1. Reservations and derogations covering restrictions of a general nature are mentioned in Table 1 above.

Table III (Cont'd)

Country	Reservations or derogations covering only restrictions by sectors	Sectors where obstacles apply specifically or more severely to non-resident investors	Sectors closed to foreign investment due to public or privately operated (or mixed) monopolies
PORTUGAL(1)			**Public monopolies** - banking and insurance (with exceptions) - production and distribution of electricity, gas and water for public use - telegraph, telephone and postal services - air and rail transport - operation of sea and air ports - war material industries - oil and petrochemical industries - steel production - fertilizers - cement
SPAIN(1)	Limited reservation which applies to investment in the film and information industries and in other defined sectors of the economy which would raise the aggregate non-resident participation of the capital of individual enterprises to more than 50 per cent or 25 per cent as the case may be and to the purchase by resident or non-resident foreigners of rural property whose area exceeds 4 hectares of irrigable land or 20 hectares of non-irrigable land.	Special restrictions apply in the following sectors: - national defence and armament - nuclear industries - public services - air transport - shipping - broadcasting - mining - banks - film industries - newspapers and news agencies - concessions for the exploitation of water resources - casinos	**Public monopolies** - railways - telegraph, telephone and postal services **Private monopolies** - Sale of duty free goods **Mixed monopolies** - oil industries - tobacco - insurance (Spanish Export Credit Insurance Company)
SWEDEN	Limited reservation which applies to the transaction only and only to the extent to which there are limitations on the right of non-residents to engage in certain activities or to acquire, own or lease certain types of property.	<u>Shipping</u> in Swedish inland waterways. <u>Domestic road transport services</u> by non-residents is restricted. Foreign <u>banks</u> may not, in principle operate in Sweden. They may, after a special permit open representative offices in Sweden. <u>Shares in banking companies</u> may be acquired only by Swedish citizens or Swedish-controlled corporations. In principle, only Swedish <u>insurance companies</u> may engage in insurance operations in Sweden. Foreign insurance companies may however receive a concession in certain fields through a general agent. Services with regard to creditworthiness information may only be carried out by Swedish entities. <u>Defence</u> Foreign-controlled enterprises are in principle not allowed to produce war-munitions within Sweden. <u>Public transport</u> Domestic air transport services may only be operated by Swedish aircraft or aircraft belonging to states with which Sweden has concluded an agreement on the right to fly over Swedish territory (according to the so-called Chicago Agreement). Swedish vessels or parts thereof may not be assigned or leased to foreign entities without a special permit.	**Public monopolies** - telegraph, telephone and postal services - television and radio broadcasting - export, import and distribution of alcoholic beverages - retail sale of pharmaceutical products - employment services (labour exchange) - rail transport services - football pools, state lotteries with money prizes and totalizer
SWITZERLAND		<u>Air transport</u> Aircraft may not be entered in the Swiss register if it is not entirely owned by Swiss nationals or companies registered under Swiss law and having their head-office in Switzerland. Aircraft belonging to a commercial firm or a co-operative whose business is the carriage of persons or goods by air may be entered in the Swiss register only if the company is neither financially nor in any other manner influenced by foreign interests.	**Public monopolies** - Passenger transport on regular schedules by ships, cars, teleferic or similar installations (concessions may be granted to private enterprises) - Telephone, telegraph and postal services - Production and import of alcoholic beverages (concessions may be granted to private enterprises) - Import of flour - Production, sale and import of gunpowder.

1. Reservations and derogations covering restrictions of a general nature are mentioned in Table I above.

Table III (Cont'd)

Country	Reservations or derogations covering only restrictions by sectors	Sectors where obstacles apply specifically or more severely to non-resident investors	Sectors closed to foreign investment due to public or privately operated (or mixed) monopolies
SWITZERLAND (Cont'd)		Admission of foreign firms for the commercial carriage of persons or goods by air on a regular schedule is regulated by international agreements. In the absence of such agreements, concessions may be granted provided the foreign firm is legally domiciled in Switzerland. Authorisation is required for foreign firms to run commercial flights outside regularly scheduled services including any class of professional flights other than flights on a regular schedule. International agreements remain valid. Authorisation may be refused if contrary to Switzerland's essential interests or in the absence of reciprocity. Maritime transport For a private company to register a ship carrying persons or goods in the Swiss shipping register, its capital and its bodies of administration and management must be in Swiss hands. Railways The administration of a foreign firm running a railway company must have a majority of Swiss nationals permanently resident in Switzerland - a permanent representative permanently resident in Switzerland must be appointed. Transmission of liquid or gazeous fuels A concession for the construction and operation of an installation crossing the national frontier may only be granted to Swiss nationals permanently resident in Switzerland, to Swiss public corporations or to Swiss corporate bodies which are clearly not controlled through capital ownership or by any other means, in a unilateral manner by foreign interests. Banking Banks under foreign control can only set up in Switzerland if - in addition to conditions applying equally to Swiss banks - the following conditions are fulfilled: there must be reciprocity on the part of the foreign State; the business name must not give the impression that the bank is a Swiss one; the bank must adhere to Swiss monetary and credit policy. These requirements equally apply to head offices, branches or agencies of a foreign-owned or controlled bank or to permanent representatives of a foreign bank. A majority of members of the management of such banks must have their permanent residence in Switzerland. Those who are foreign residents may only sign jointly with another person resident in Switzerland who is also a member of the management. Insurance companies A foreign insurance company - i.e. a company having its head office abroad - can only obtain a licence to carry out direct insurance business if - in addition to conditions applying equally to Swiss companies - the following conditions are fulfilled: It must be licensed to carry out insurance business in its country of origin and must have carried out such business for at least three years; have an office in Switzerland for all business carried out in Switzerland and appoint a general agent permanently resident in Switzerland and have competence in the field of insurance to actually manage that office. The appointment of the general agent is subject to approval by the federal office of private insurance. Foreign insurance companies are moreover subject to special regulations as regards legal deposits.	Privately operated or mixed monopolies - Air transport (for certain flights of general interest) - Air safety services - Radio and television broadcasting There are moreover a number of cantonal monopolies, e.g. for fishing, hunting, mining, salt, fire insurance.

Table III (Cont'd)

Country	Reservations or derogations covering only restrictions by sectors	Sectors where obstacles apply specifically or more severely to non-resident investors	Sectors closed to foreign investment due to public or privately operated (or mixed) monopolies
SWITZERLAND (Cont'd)		**Oil production** In cantons adhering to the Agreement on the prospection and extraction of oil, concessions for the prospection and extraction are granted only if at least three-quarters of the share capital of the company extracting oil is in Swiss hands. **Water power** Concessions for the use of water power are only granted to Swiss nationals permanently resident in Switzerland or corporate bodies having their headquarters in Swizterland. At least two-thirds of the members of the board of management must be Swiss nationals and be permanently resident in Switzerland. Conventions on the use of frontier water courses remain valid. **Atomic energy** Granting of authorisation by Federal authorities for constructing or operating a nuclear installation may be subject to the condition that the applicant be a Swiss citizen living in Switzerland. If authorisation is sought by a corporate body, the authorities may require that its headquarters be in Switzerland and that it should be under Swiss control.	
UNITED KINGDOM		**Air transport** Air transport licences are not granted by the Civil Aviation Authority to applicants who are not U.K. nationals or a body incorporated in the U.K. (or certain overseas territories) and controlled by U.K. nationals unless the Secretary of State consents to the grant of the licence. **Broadcasting** Individuals who are not normally resident in the United Kingdm, the Channel Islands and the Isle of Man; corporate bodies incorporated outside these territories; and corporate bodies controlled by persons not normally resident in the British Islands are disqualified from having a controlling interest in any programme companies providing programmes for transmission by the Independent Broadcasting Authority's transmitters. New legislation now before Parliament proposes to amend this list of disqualified persons to exclude from it any nationals of Member States of the European Communities who are ordinarily resident within the European Community and any corporate body which has its registered head-office or principal place of business within the European Community. **Insurance** Insurance companies whose head-office is not in a Member State of the European Communities are placed under different requirements in respect of the solvency limits to be achieved and maintained. They are required to deposit with the Accountant General of the Supreme Court certain set sums. They are also required to meet certain conditions on seeking authorisation to write general insurance business and to continue to do so after authorisation has been granted.	**Public monopolies** Postal services and telecommunications systems (the Post Office has exclusive rights over the collection, carriage and delivery of mail and the exclusive right to run all telecommunications' services), electricity production and supply (restricted to nationalised statutory electricity boards), rail services (controlled by British Rail), water distribution (controlled by the area water boards) and gas production and supply (controlled by the British Gas Corporation). **Privately operated (or mixed) monopolies** **Coal production** Privately owned mines may only operate with a licence from the National Coal Board. In exchange for the licence to carry out mining activities, private mines must pay a royalty to the National Coal Board. Their number of employees and the annual output of private mines is limited by statute.
UNITED STATES	Limited reservation which applies only to certain statutory provisions which prohibit immediate direct investments by aliens in enterprises engaged in fresh water shipping, domestic radio communications and domestic air transport, or which limit to 25 per cent alien participation in corporations engaged in such enterprises, and	A foreign or foreign-controlled enterprise may not: - be issued permits for intra-United States air commerce or navigation; - engage in radio or television broadcasting, unless the Federal Communications Commission finds the grant of a licence to be in the public interest; - engage in operations involving the utilisation or production of atomic energy; - acquire rights-of-way for oil pipelines, or leases, or interests therein for mining coal, oil, or certain	**Public monopolies** None **Privately operated monopolies** The Communications Satellite Corporation was established by the Communications Satellite Act of 1962 as a private corporation to establish and operate a commercial satellite system. Under the Act, not more than an aggregate of 20 per cent of the shares of its stock which are

34

Table III (Cont'd)

Country	Reservations or derogations covering only restrictions by sectors	Sectors where obstacles apply specifically or more severely to non-resident investors	Sectors closed to foreign investment due to public or privately operated (or mixed) monopolies
UNITED STATES (Cont'd)	which place certain other requirements on investments by aliens in enterprises engaged in coastal shipping, hydro-electric power production, other forms of communications and the utilisation or	other minerals on federal lands, other than the continental shelf, if the foreign investor's home country does not permit such mineral leasing to U.S.-controlled enterprises; - engage in coastal shipping, dredging, or salvaging. A foreign-controlled enterprise operating in the United States must meet certain requirements in order to: - obtain access to hard mineral deposits such as uranium in lands belonging to the United States; - obtain the necessary documentation for vessels to fish in the U.S. fishing conservation zone; - obtain a licence to operate as a customs broker (requirement relating to management). A number of States prohibit or limit the ownership of agricultural land by non-resident foreigners or foreign corporations. Establishment of a bank or opening of a branch or agency by a foreign bank can be effected at the federal or state level. At the state level, this requires approval from the authorities of that state, this approval being sometimes subject to citizenship requirements or to reciprocity. Foreign and domestic insurance companies which are not resident of the State concerned must obtain a licence to open a branch in a State. Licensing requirements may differ from those of residents of the State on the following points: ownership limitations, deposit requirements, licence renewals, investment requirements and capital requirements. Also the activities of foreign branches are limited in many States. In addition, non-U.S. insurers may be subject to reciprocity provisions.	offered to the public may be held by aliens, foreign governments, or foreign-owned, registered or controlled corporations.

OECD SALES AGENTS
DÉPOSITAIRES DES PUBLICATIONS DE L'OCDE

ARGENTINA – ARGENTINE
Carlos Hirsch S.R.L., Florida 165, 4° Piso (Galería Guemes)
1333 BUENOS AIRES, Tel. 33.1787.2391 y 30.7122
AUSTRALIA – AUSTRALIE
Australia and New Zealand Book Company Pty, Ltd.,
10 Aquatic Drive, Frenchs Forest, N.S.W. 2086
P.O. Box 459, BROOKVALE, N.S.W. 2100
AUSTRIA – AUTRICHE
OECD Publications and Information Center
4 Simrockstrasse 5300 BONN. Tel. (0228) 21.60.45
Local Agent/Agent local :
Gerold and Co., Graben 31, WIEN 1. Tel. 52.22.35
BELGIUM – BELGIQUE
LCLS
35, avenue de Stalingrad, 1000 BRUXELLES. Tel. 02.512.89.74
BRAZIL – BRÉSIL
Mestre Jou S.A., Rua Guaipa 518,
Caixa Postal 24090, 05089 SAO PAULO 10. Tel. 261.1920
Rua Senador Dantas 19 s/205-6, RIO DE JANEIRO GB.
Tel. 232.07.32
CANADA
Renouf Publishing Company Limited,
2182 St. Catherine Street West,
MONTRÉAL, Que. H3H 1M7. Tel. (514)937.3519
OTTAWA, Ont. K1P 5A6, 61 Sparks Street
DENMARK – DANEMARK
Munksgaard Export and Subscription Service
35, Nørre Søgade
DK 1370 KØBENHAVN K. Tel. +45.1.12.85.70
FINLAND – FINLANDE
Akateeminen Kirjakauppa
Keskuskatu 1, 00100 HELSINKI 10. Tel. 65.11.22
FRANCE
Bureau des Publications de l'OCDE,
2 rue André-Pascal, 75775 PARIS CEDEX 16. Tel. (1) 524.81.67
Principal correspondant :
13602 AIX-EN-PROVENCE : Librairie de l'Université.
Tel. 26.18.08
GERMANY – ALLEMAGNE
OECD Publications and Information Center
4 Simrockstrasse 5300 BONN Tel. (0228) 21.60.45
GREECE – GRÈCE
Librairie Kauffmann, 28 rue du Stade,
ATHÈNES 132. Tel. 322.21.60
HONG-KONG
Government Information Services,
Publications/Sales Section, Baskerville House,
2/F., 22 Ice House Street
ICELAND – ISLANDE
Snaebjörn Jönsson and Co., h.f.,
Hafnarstraeti 4 and 9, P.O.B. 1131, REYKJAVIK.
Tel. 13133/14281/11936
INDIA – INDE
Oxford Book and Stationery Co. :
NEW DELHI-1, Scindia House. Tel. 45896
CALCUTTA 700016, 17 Park Street. Tel. 240832
INDONESIA – INDONÉSIE
PDIN-LIPI, P.O. Box 3065/JKT., JAKARTA, Tel. 583467
IRELAND – IRLANDE
TDC Publishers – Library Suppliers
12 North Frederick Street, DUBLIN 1 Tel. 744835-749677
ITALY – ITALIE
Libreria Commissionaria Sansoni :
Via Lamarmora 45, 50121 FIRENZE. Tel. 579751
Via Bartolini 29, 20155 MILANO. Tel. 365083
Sub-depositari :
Editrice e Libreria Herder,
Piazza Montecitorio 120, 00 186 ROMA. Tel. 6794628
Libreria Hoepli, Via Hoepli 5, 20121 MILANO. Tel. 865446
Libreria Lattes, Via Garibaldi 3, 10122 TORINO. Tel. 519274
La diffusione delle edizioni OCSE è inoltre assicurata dalle migliori
librerie nelle città più importanti.
JAPAN – JAPON
OECD Publications and Information Center,
Landic Akasaka Bldg., 2-3-4 Akasaka,
Minato-ku, TOKYO 107 Tel. 586.2016
KOREA – CORÉE
Pan Korea Book Corporation,
P.O. Box n° 101 Kwangwhamun, SÉOUL. Tel. 72.7369
LEBANON – LIBAN
Documenta Scientifica/Redico,
Edison Building, Bliss Street, P.O. Box 5641, BEIRUT.
Tel. 354429 – 344425

MALAYSIA – MALAISIE
and/et SINGAPORE - SINGAPOUR
University of Malaysia Co-operative Bookshop Ltd.
P.O. Box 1127, Jalan Pantai Baru
KUALA LUMPUR. Tel. 51425, 54058, 54361
THE NETHERLANDS – PAYS-BAS
Staatsuitgeverij
Verzendboekhandel Chr. Plantijnstraat 1
Postbus 20014
2500 EA S-GRAVENAGE. Tel. nr. 070.789911
Voor bestellingen: Tel. 070.789208
NEW ZEALAND – NOUVELLE-ZÉLANDE
Publications Section,
Government Printing Office Bookshops:
AUCKLAND: Retail Bookshop: 25 Rutland Street,
Mail Orders: 85 Beach Road, Private Bag C.P.O.
HAMILTON: Retail Ward Street,
Mail Orders, P.O. Box 857
WELLINGTON: Retail: Mulgrave Street (Head Office),
Cubacade World Trade Centre
Mail Orders: Private Bag
CHRISTCHURCH: Retail: 159 Hereford Street,
Mail Orders: Private Bag
DUNEDIN: Retail: Princes Street
Mail Order: P.O. Box 1104
NORWAY – NORVÈGE
J.G. TANUM A/S Karl Johansgate 43
P.O. Box 1177 Sentrum OSLO 1. Tel. (02) 80.12.60
PAKISTAN
Mirza Book Agency, 65 Shahrah Quaid-E-Azam, LAHORE 3.
Tel. 66839
PHILIPPINES
National Book Store, Inc.
Library Services Division, P.O. Box 1934, MANILA.
Tel. Nos. 49.43.06 to 09, 40.53.45, 49.45.12
PORTUGAL
Livraria Portugal, Rua do Carmo 70-74,
1117 LISBOA CODEX. Tel. 360582/3
SPAIN – ESPAGNE
Mundi-Prensa Libros, S.A.
Castelló 37, Apartado 1223, MADRID-1. Tel. 275.46.55
Libreria Bosch, Ronda Universidad 11, BARCELONA 7.
Tel. 317.53.08, 317.53.58
SWEDEN – SUÈDE
AB CE Fritzes Kungl Hovbokhandel,
Box 16 356, S 103 27 STH, Regeringsgatan 12,
DS STOCKHOLM. Tel. 08/23.89.00
SWITZERLAND – SUISSE
OECD Publications and Information Center
4 Simrockstrasse 5300 BONN. Tel. (0228) 21.60.45
Local Agents/Agents locaux
Librairie Payot, 6 rue Grenus, 1211 GENÈVE 11. Tel. 022.31.89.50
Freihofer A.G., Weinbergstr. 109, CH-8006 ZÜRICH.
Tel. 01.363428.2
TAIWAN
Good Faith Worldwide int'l Co., Ltd.
9th floor, No. 118, Sec. 2
Chung Hsiao E. Road
TAIPEI. Tel. 391.7396/391.7397
THAILAND – THAILANDE
Suksit Siam Co., Ltd., 1715 Rama IV Rd,
Samyan, BANGKOK 5. Tel. 2511630
TURKEY – TURQUIE
Kültur Yayinlari Is-Türk Ltd. Sti.
Atatürk Bulvari No : 77/B
KIZILAY/ANKARA. Tel. 17 02 66
Dolmabahce Cad. No : 29
BESIKTAS/ISTANBUL. Tel. 60 71 88
UNITED KINGDOM – ROYAUME-UNI
H.M. Stationery Office, P.O.B. 569,
LONDON SE1   9NH. Tel. 01.928.6977, Ext. 410 or
49 High Holborn, LONDON WC1V 6 HB (personal callers)
Branches at: EDINBURGH, BIRMINGHAM, BRISTOL,
MANCHESTER, CARDIFF, BELFAST.
UNITED STATES OF AMERICA – ÉTATS-UNIS
OECD Publications and Information Center, Suite 1207,
1750 Pennsylvania Ave., N.W. WASHINGTON, D.C.20006 – 4582
Tel. (202) 724.1857
VENEZUELA
Libreria del Este, Avda. F. Miranda 52, Edificio Galipan,
CARACAS 106. Tel. 32.23.01/33.26.04/33.24.73
YUGOSLAVIA – YOUGOSLAVIE
Jugoslovenska Knjiga, Terazije 27, P.O.B. 36, BEOGRAD.
Tel. 621.992

Les commandes provenant de pays où l'OCDE n'a pas encore désigné de dépositaire peuvent être adressées à :
OCDE, Bureau des Publications, 2, rue André-Pascal, 75775 PARIS CEDEX 16.

Orders and inquiries from countries where sales agents have not yet been appointed may be sent to:
OECD, Publications Office, 2 rue André-Pascal, 75775 PARIS CEDEX 16.

OECD PUBLICATIONS, 2, rue André-Pascal, 75775 PARIS CEDEX 16 - No. 42241 1982
PRINTED IN FRANCE
(21 82 06 1) ISBN 92-64-12344-X